FLEUR–DE–LYS COLORING BOOK

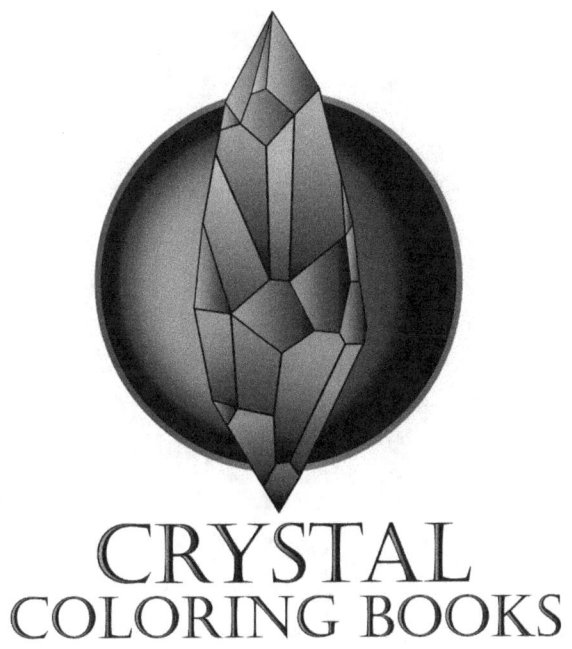

CRYSTAL COLORING BOOKS

ISBN-13: 978-1984955937
ISBN-10: 1984955934

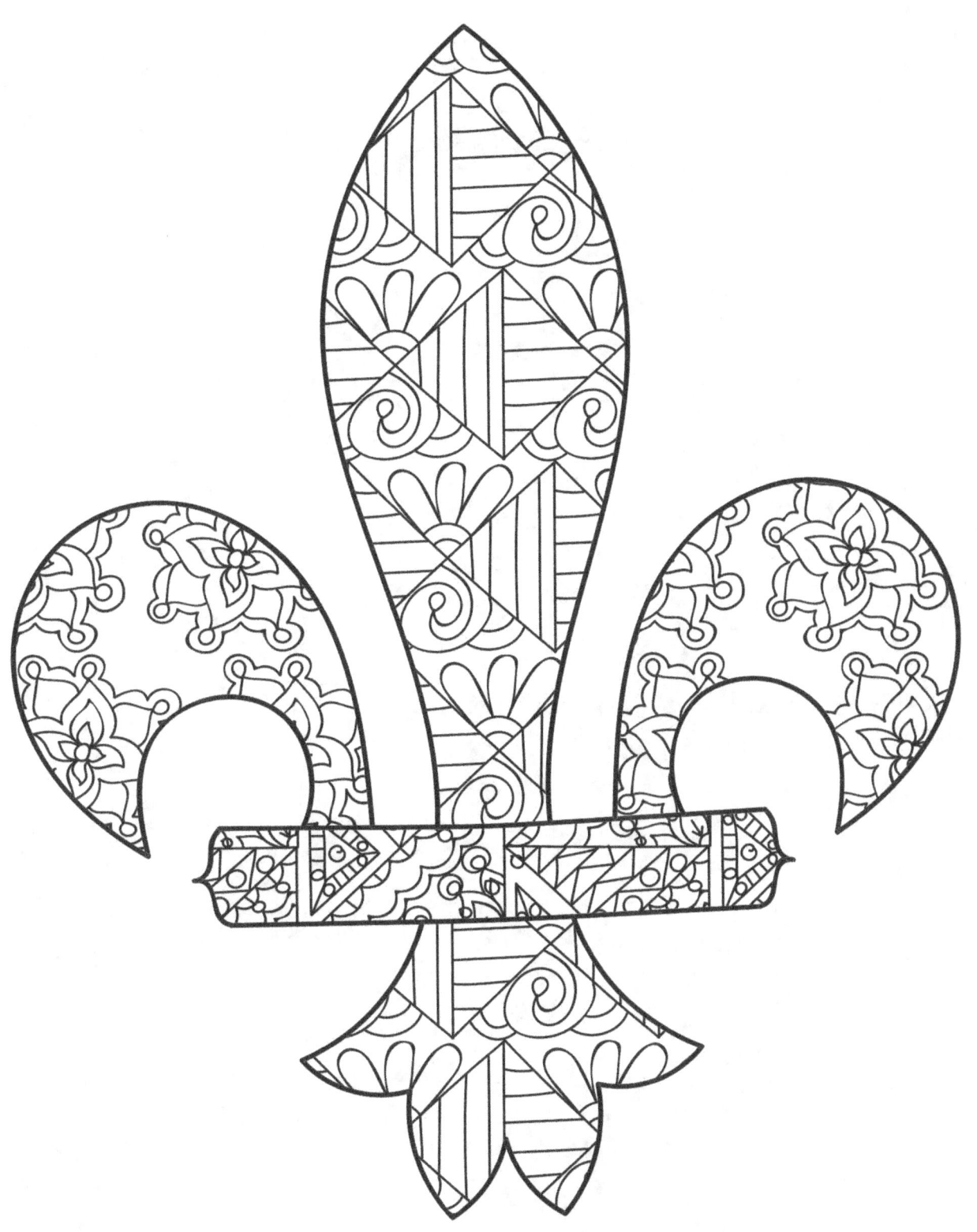

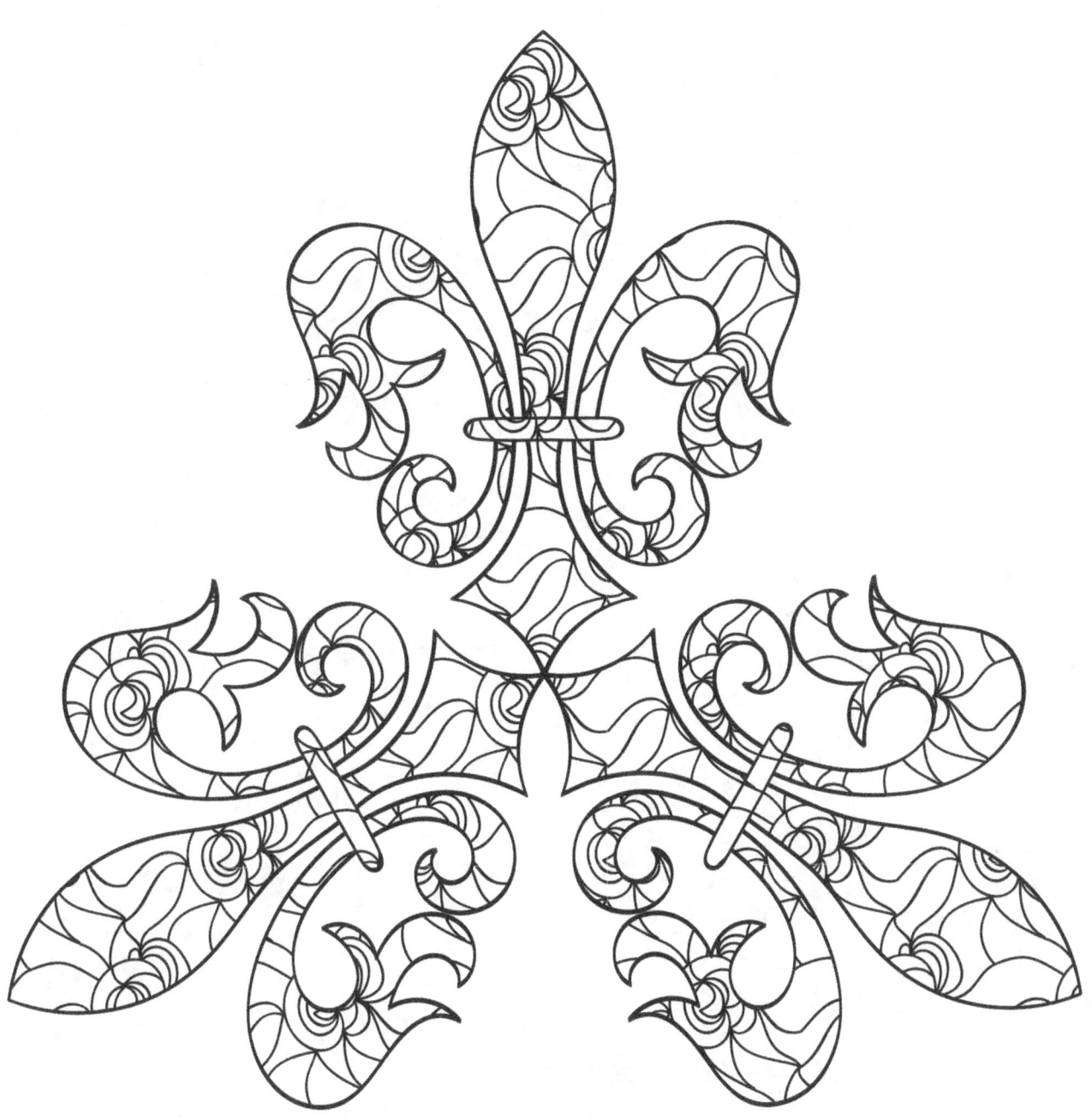

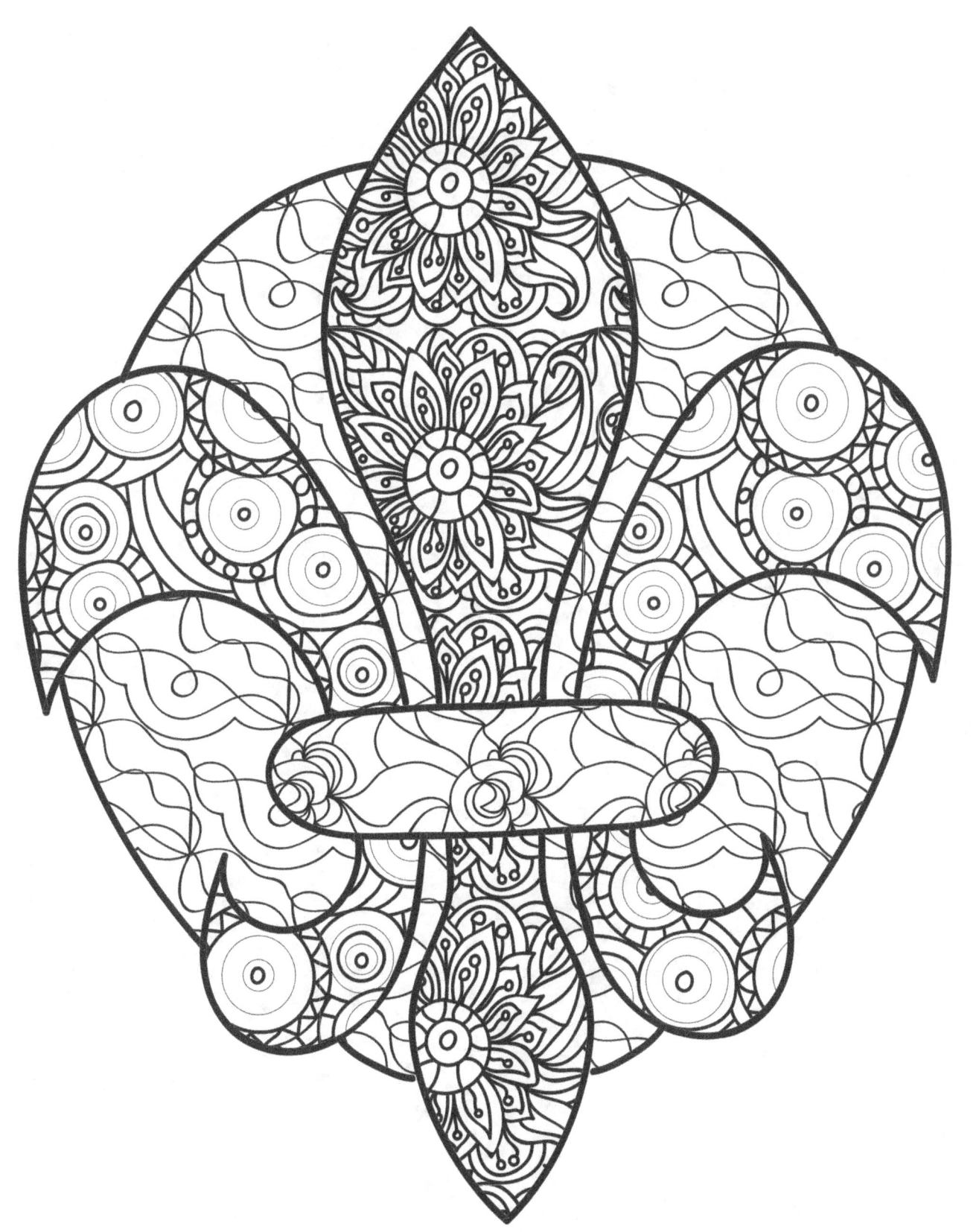

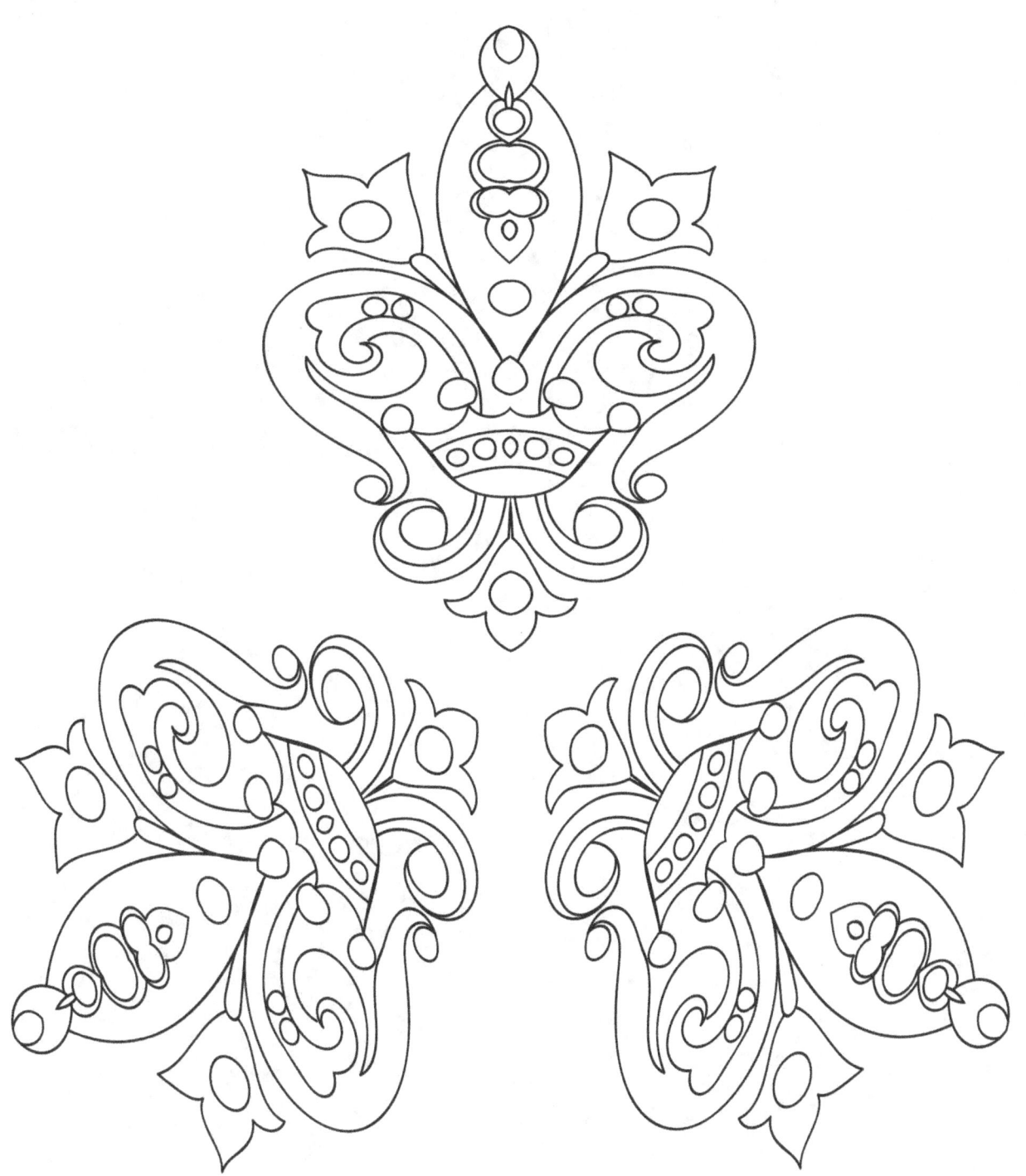

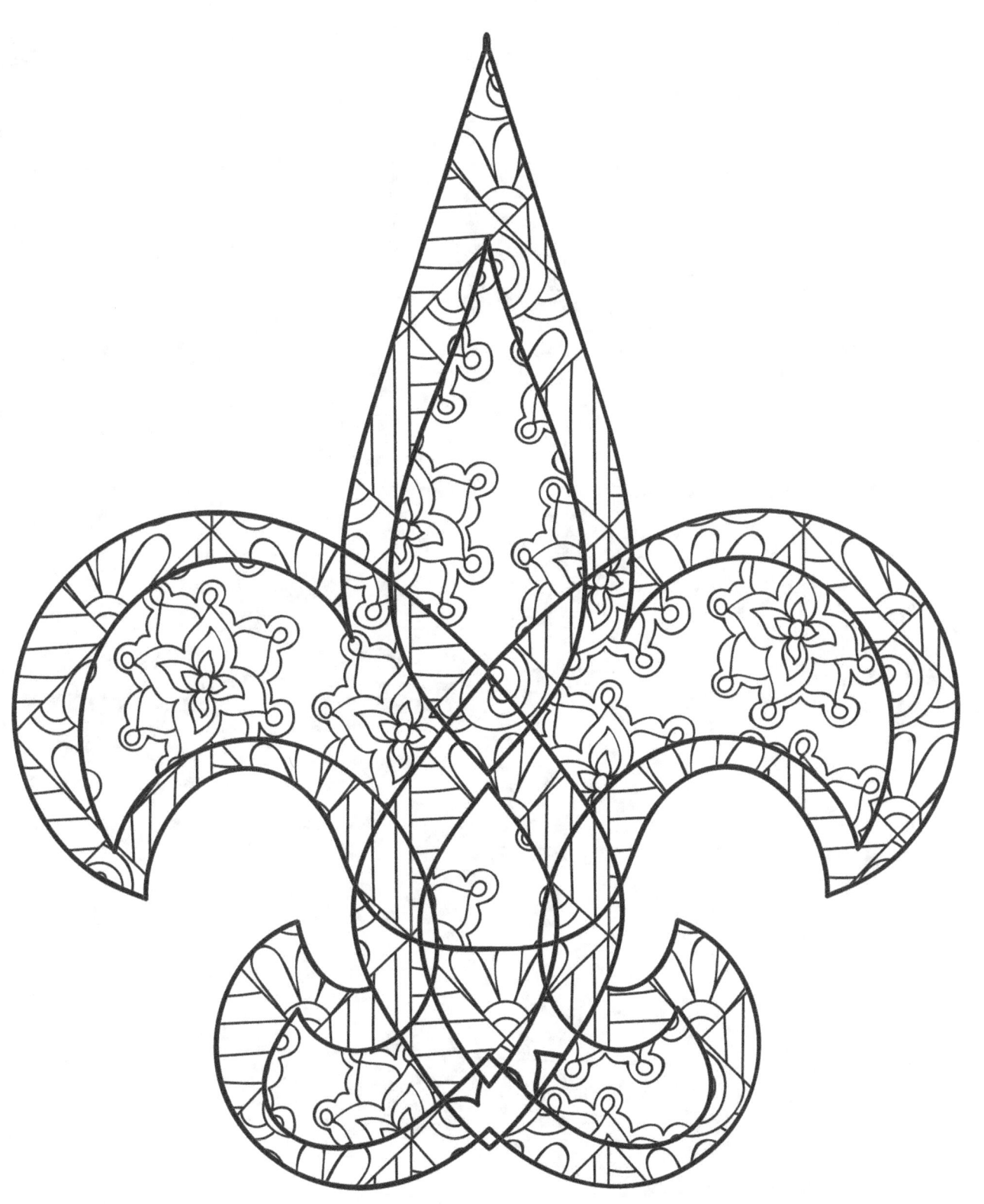

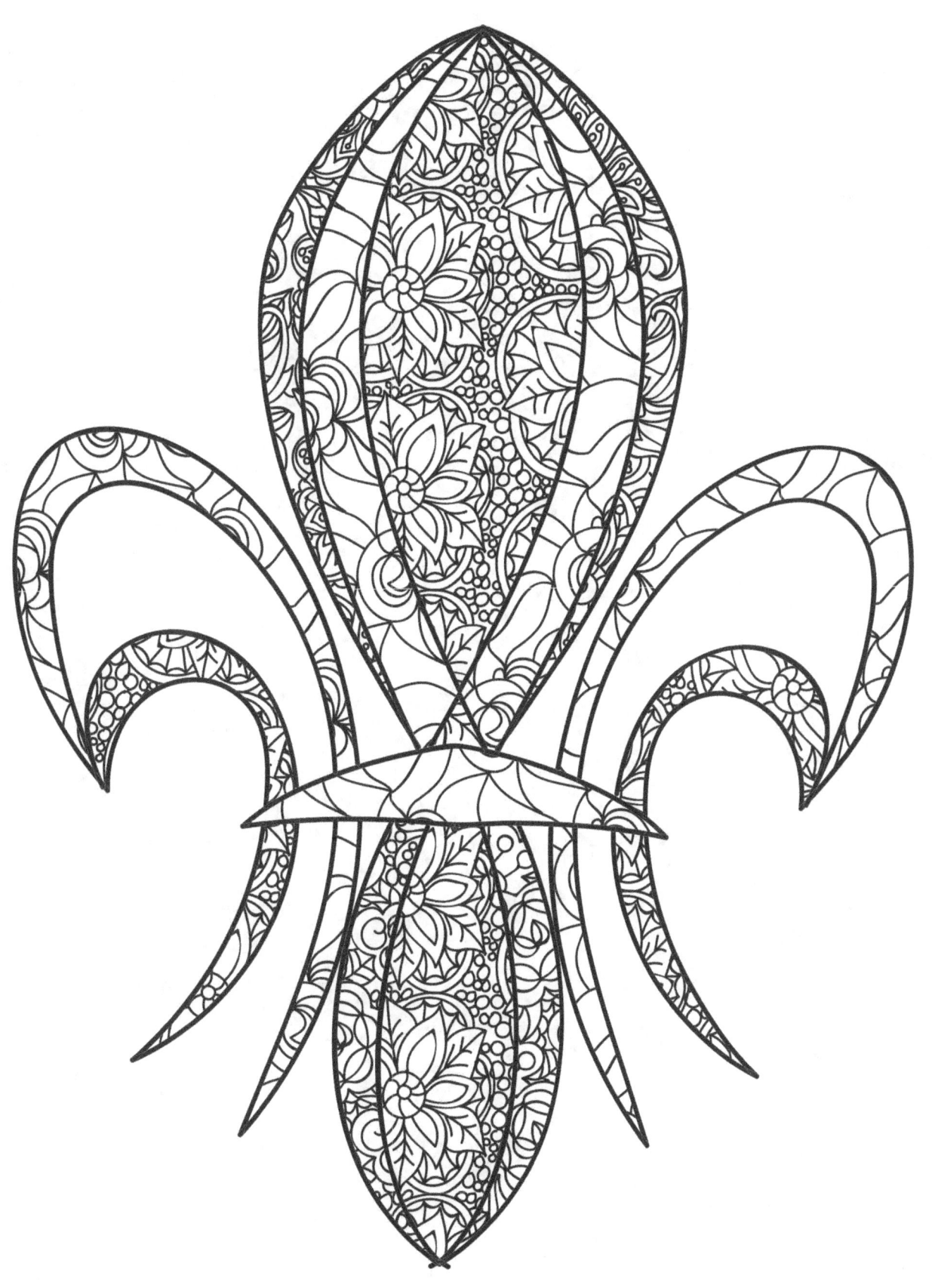

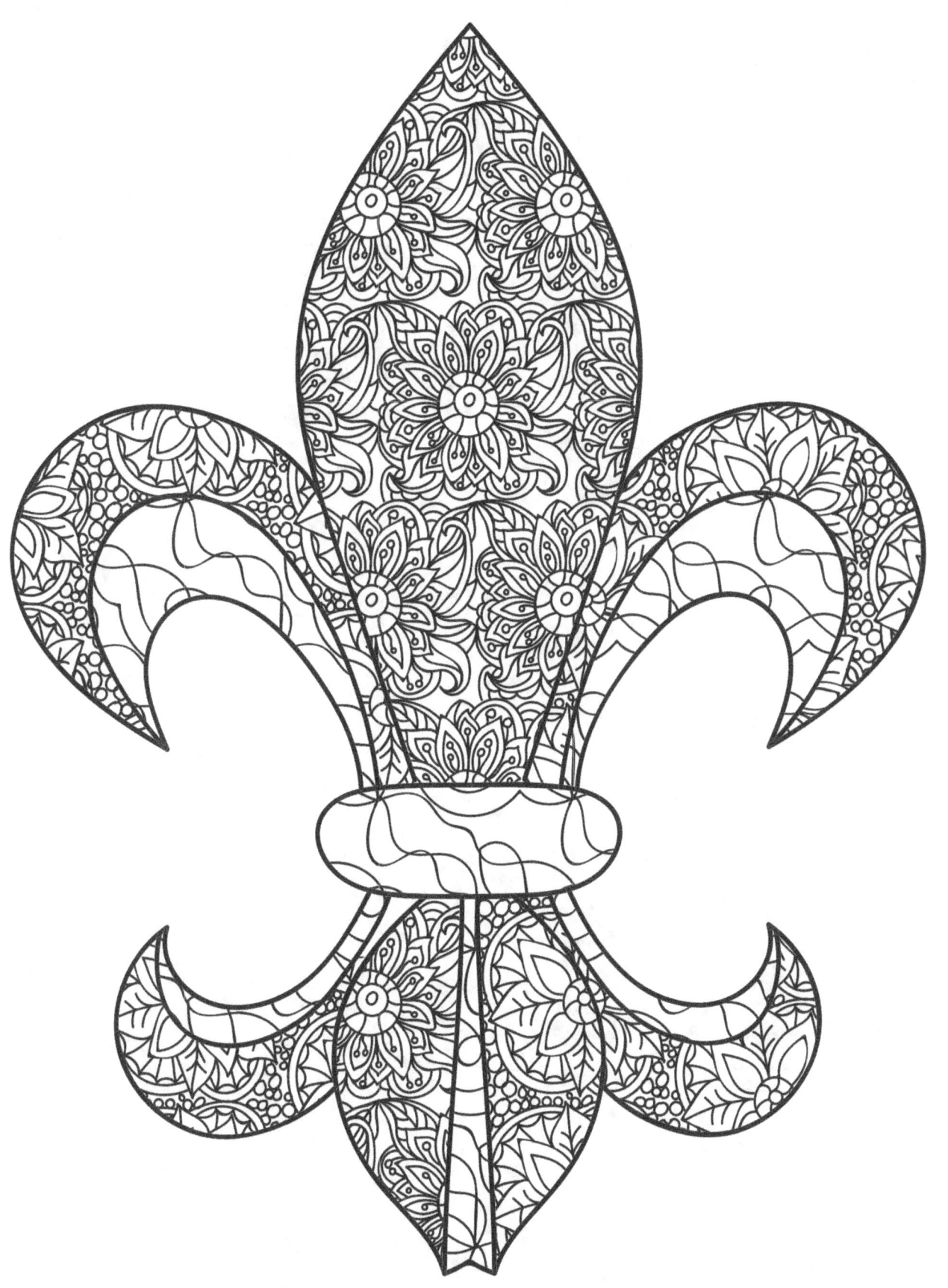

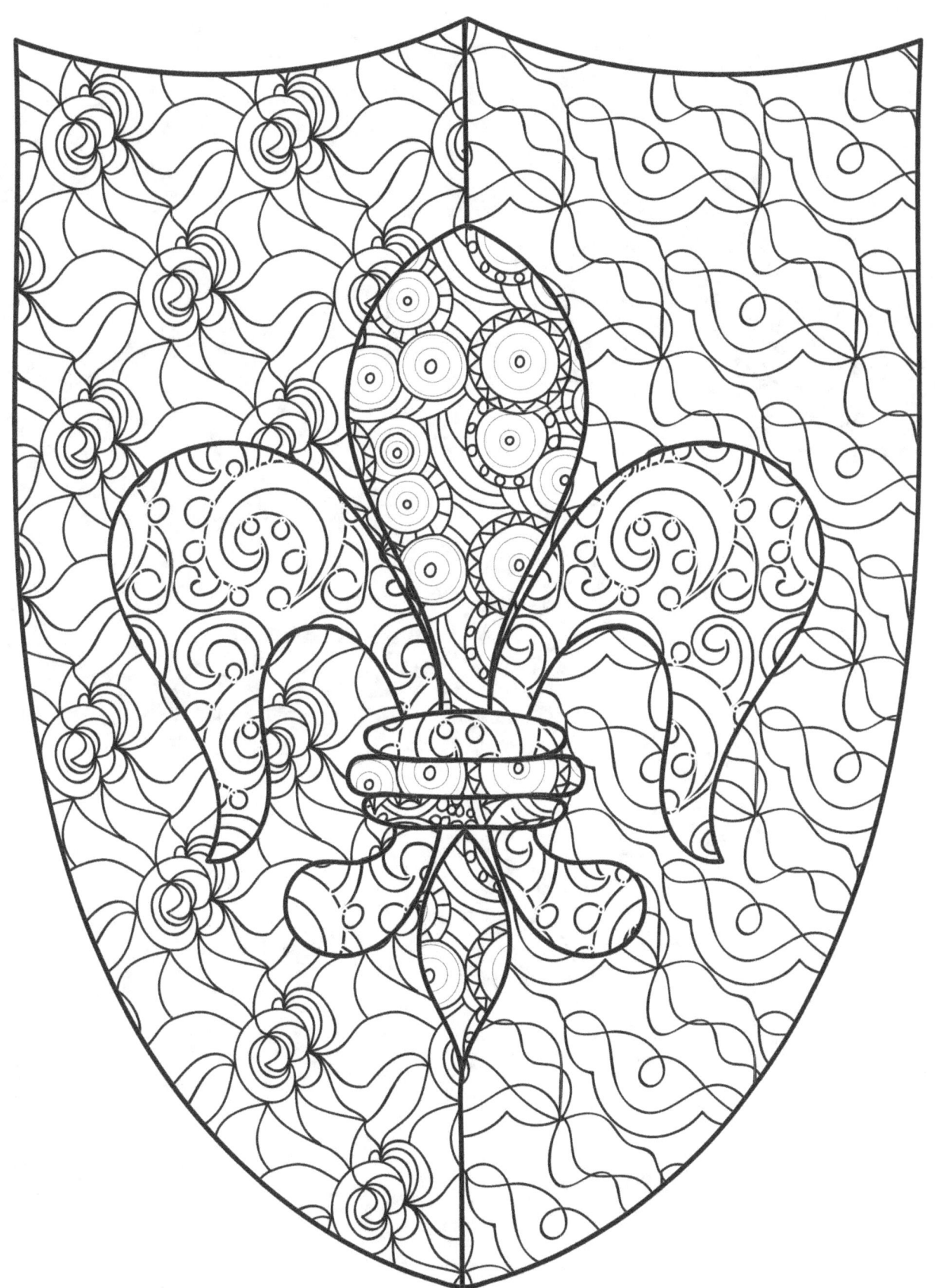

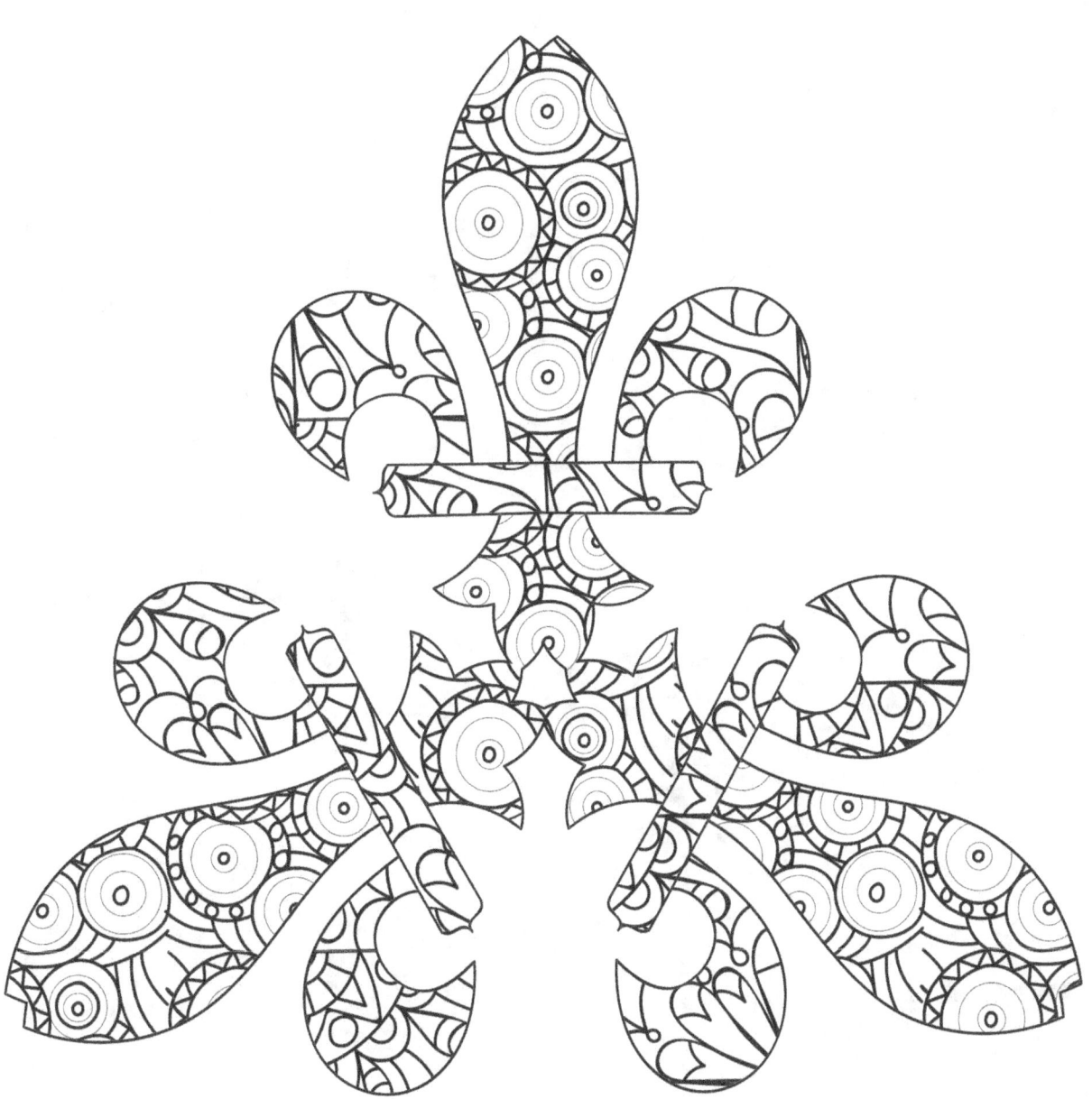

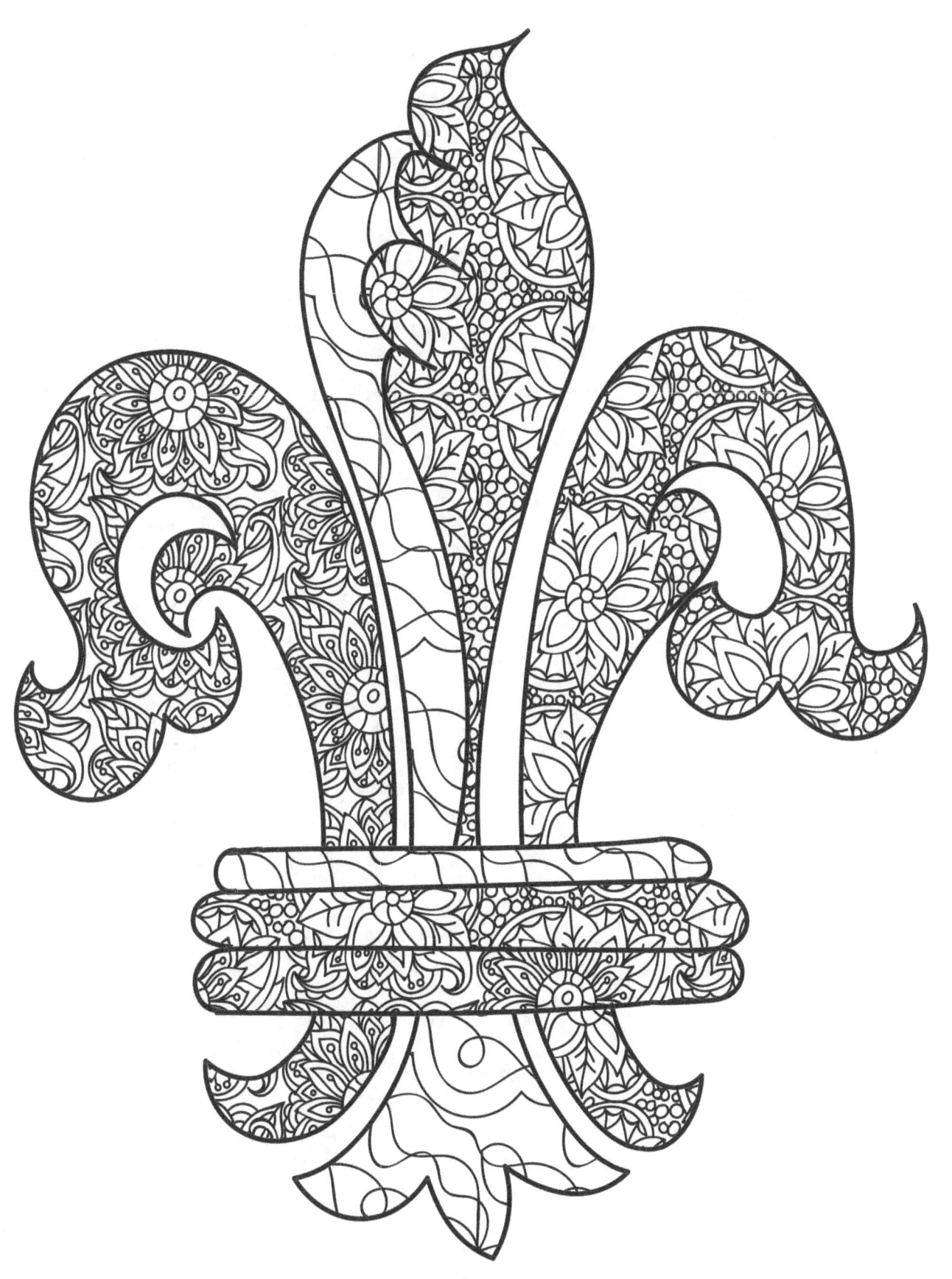

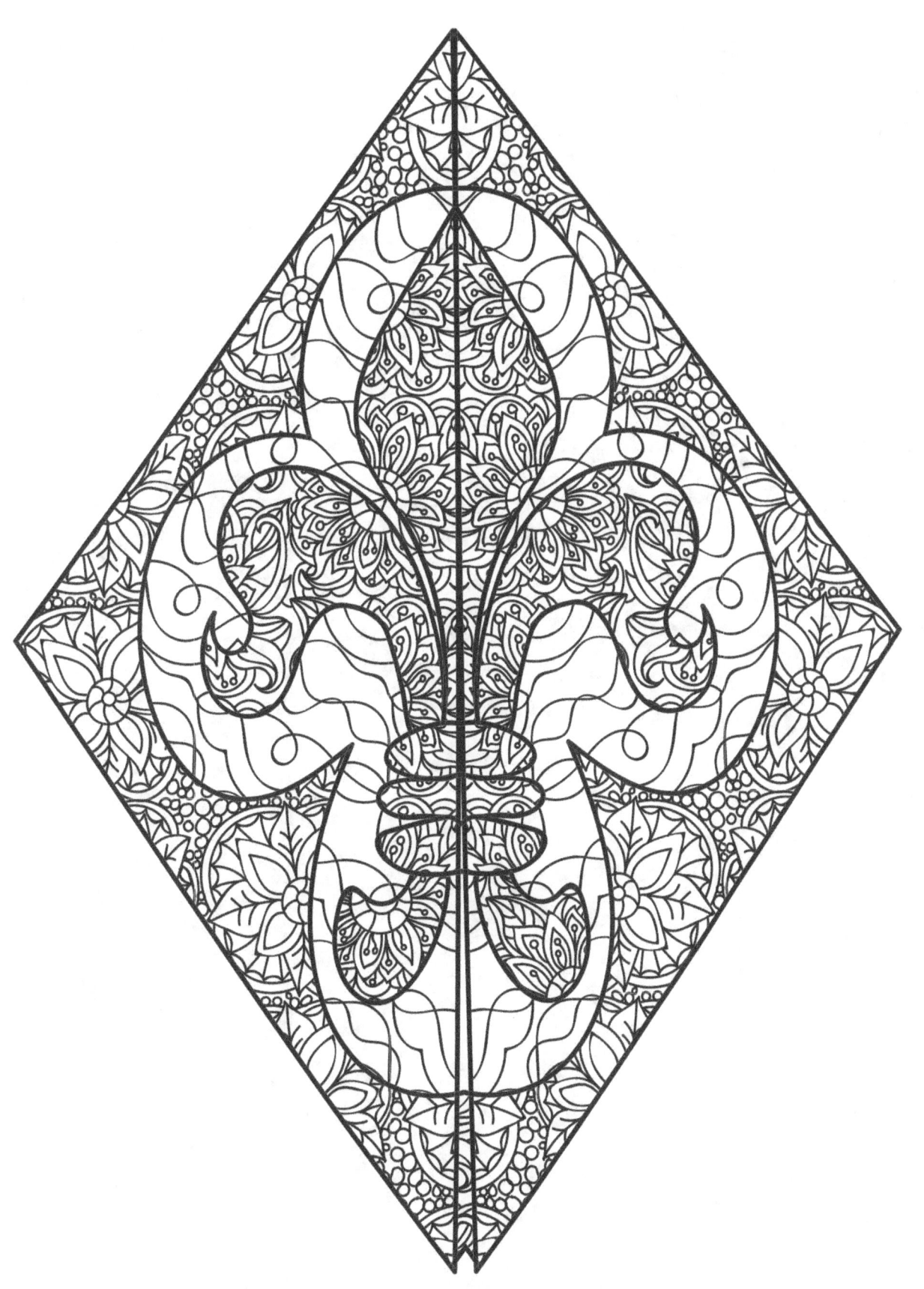

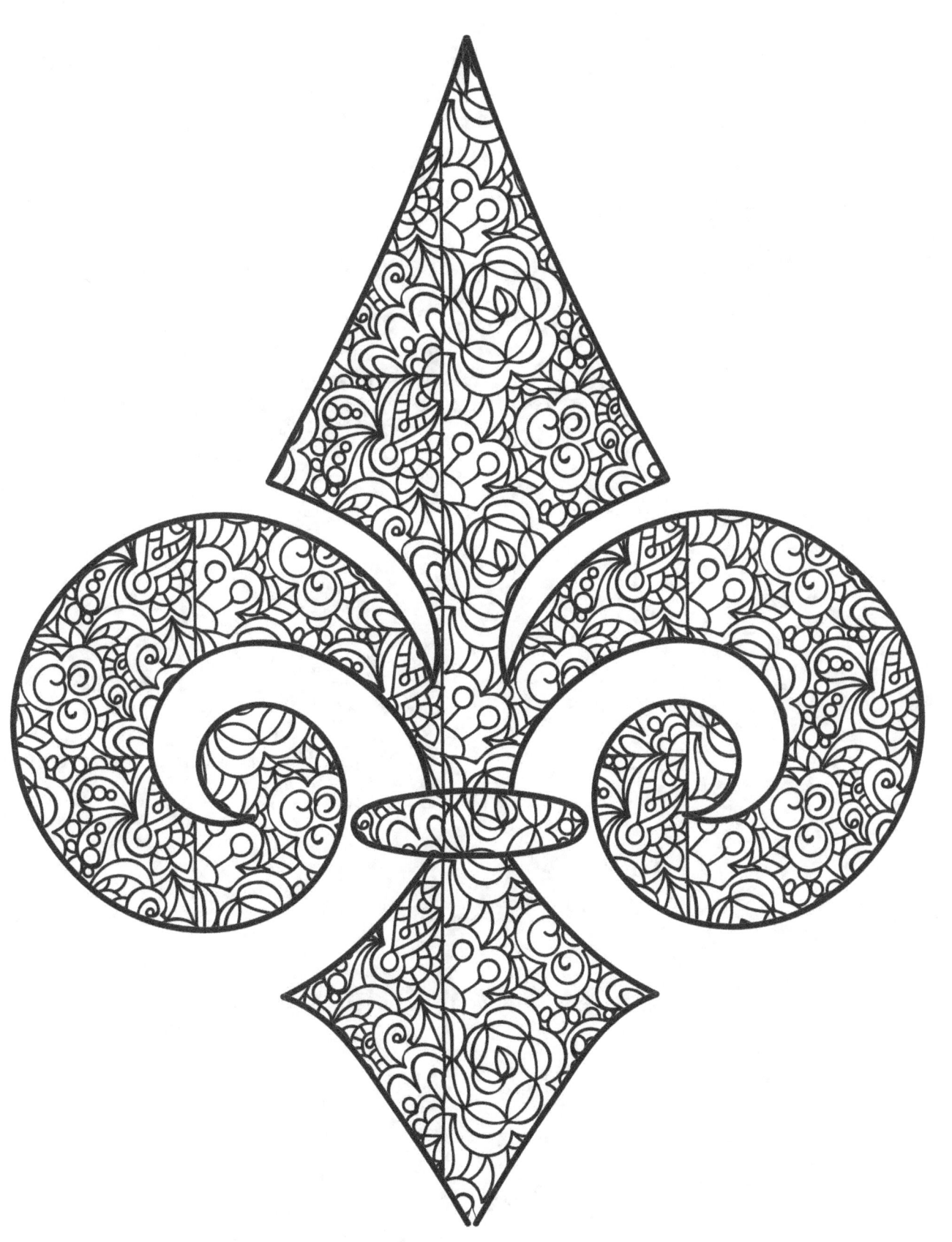

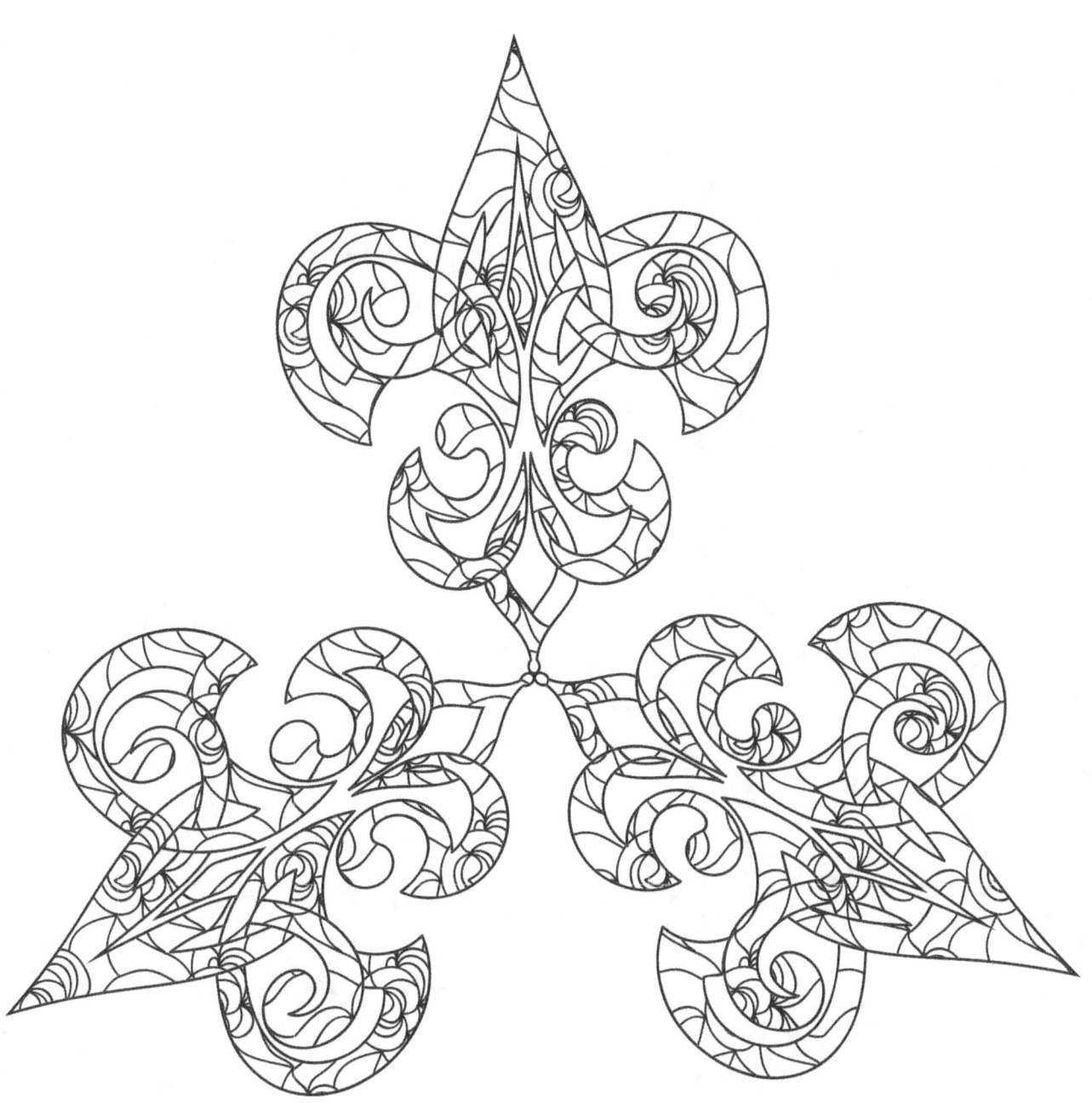

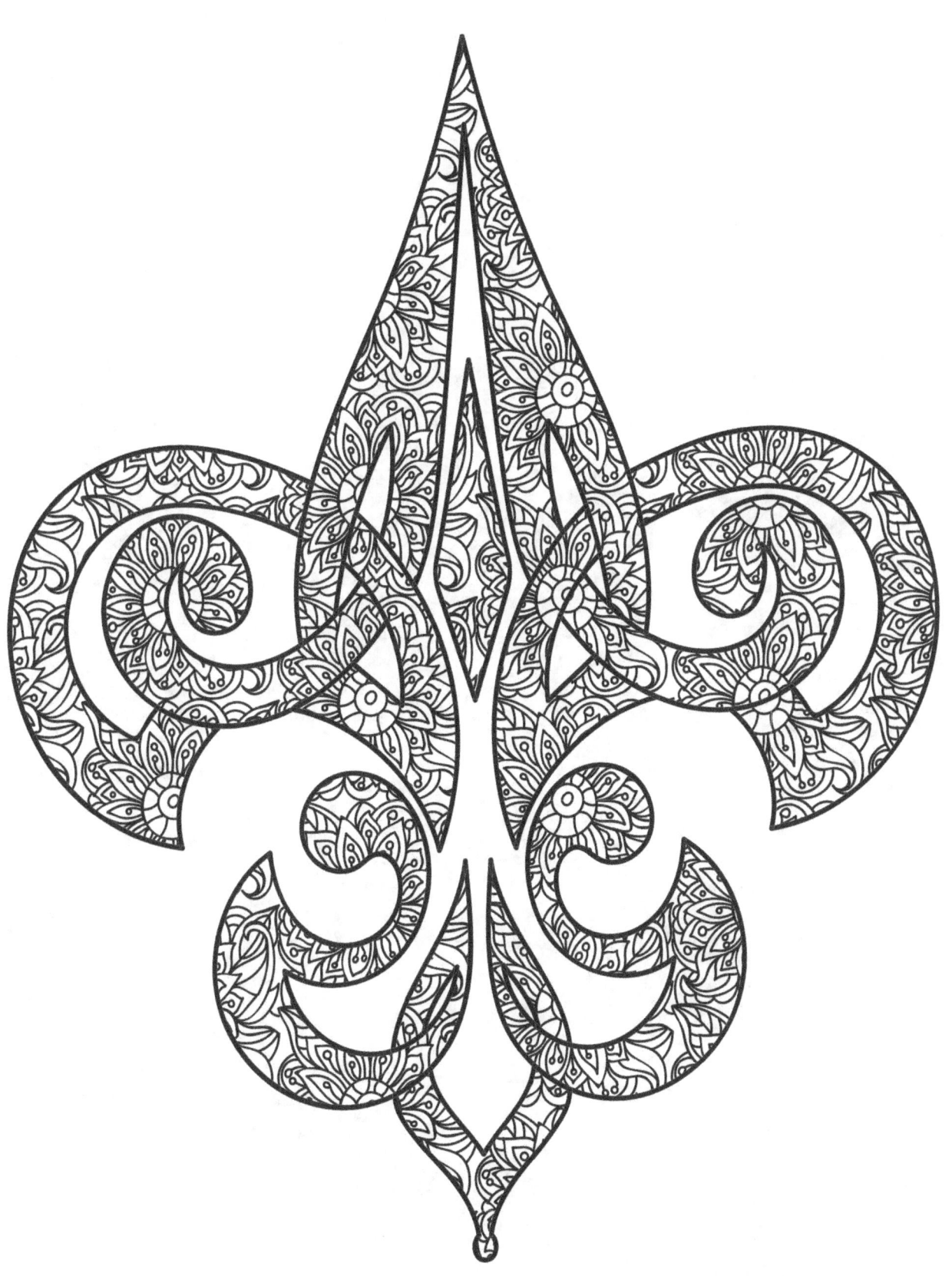

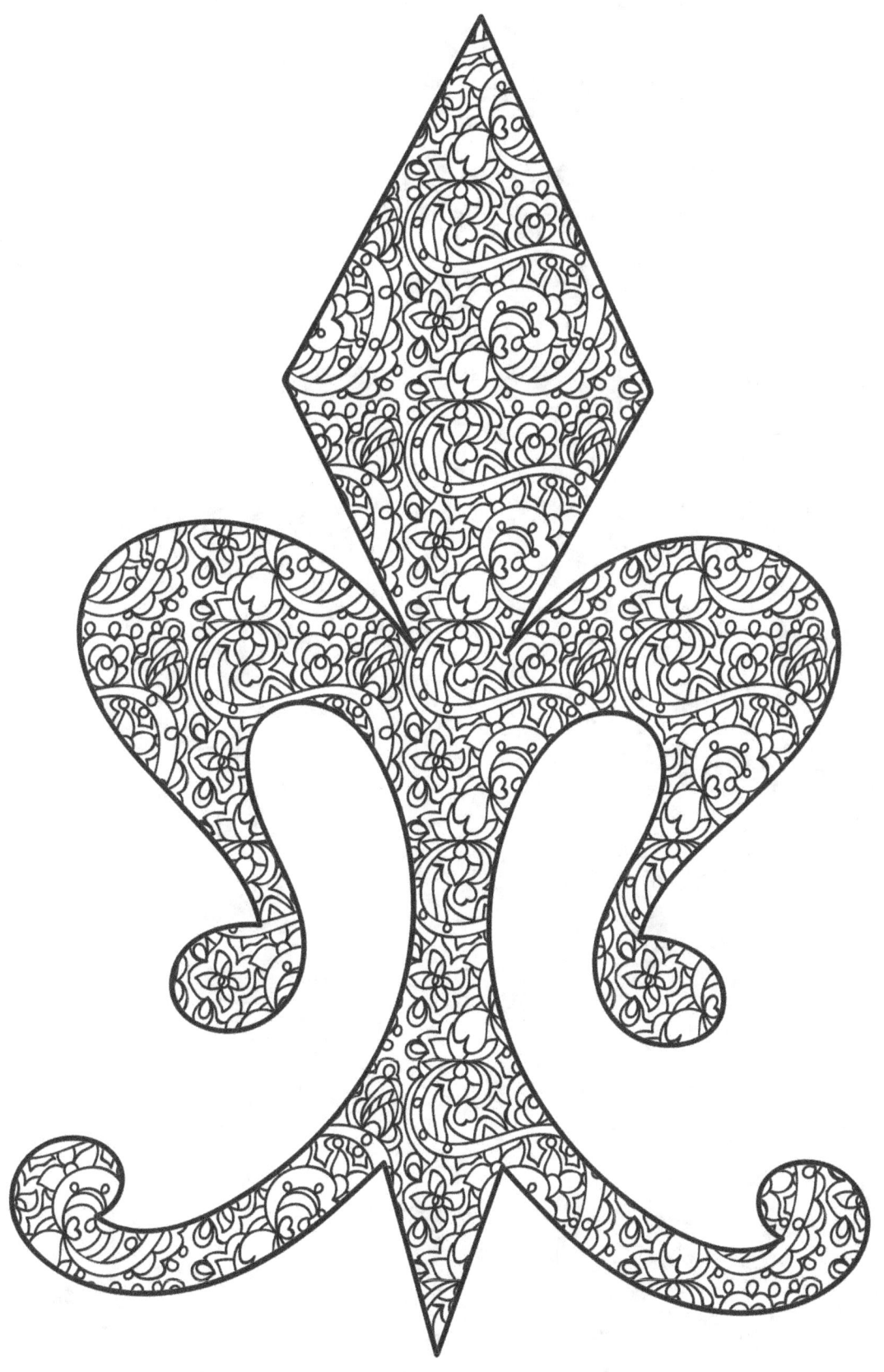

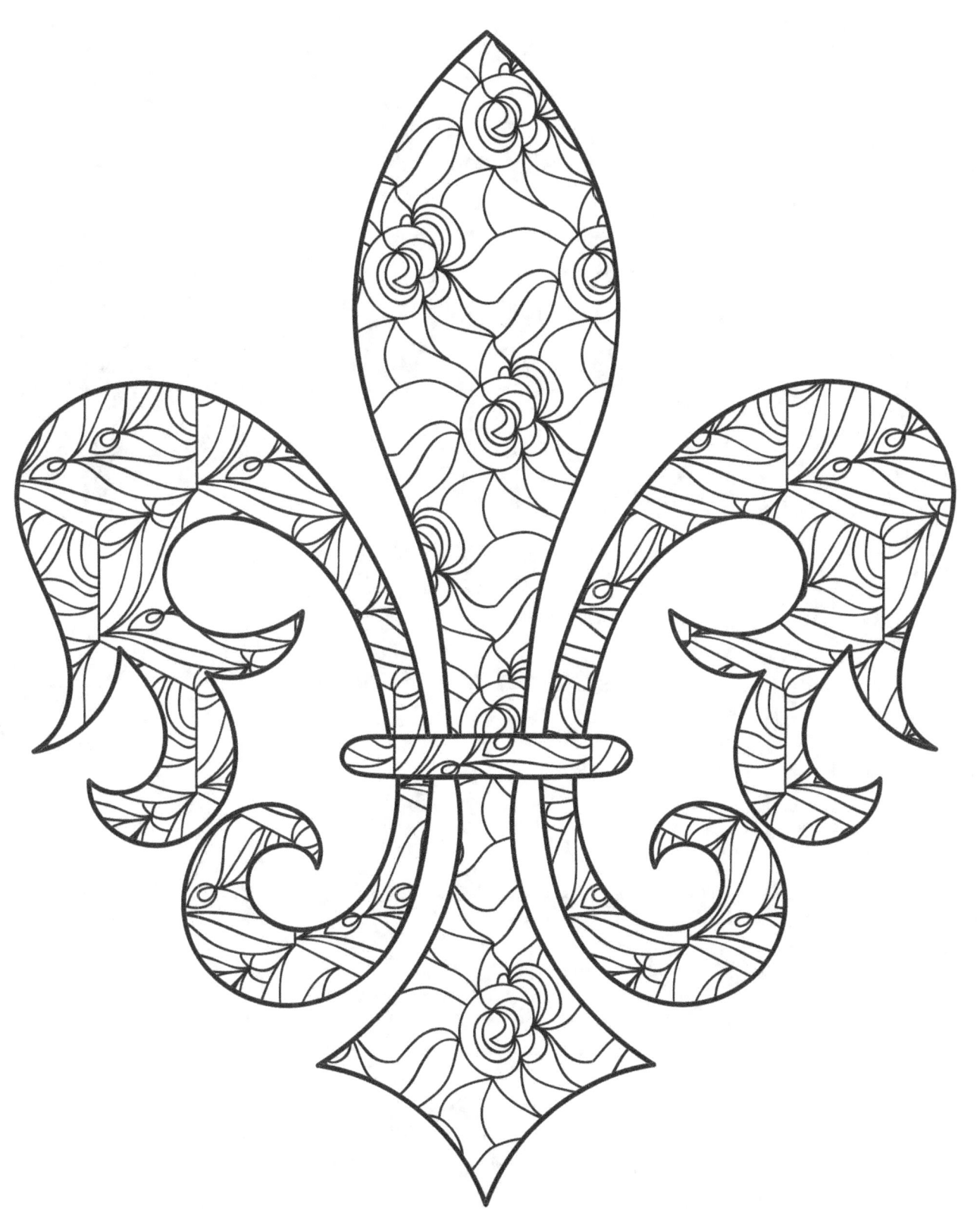

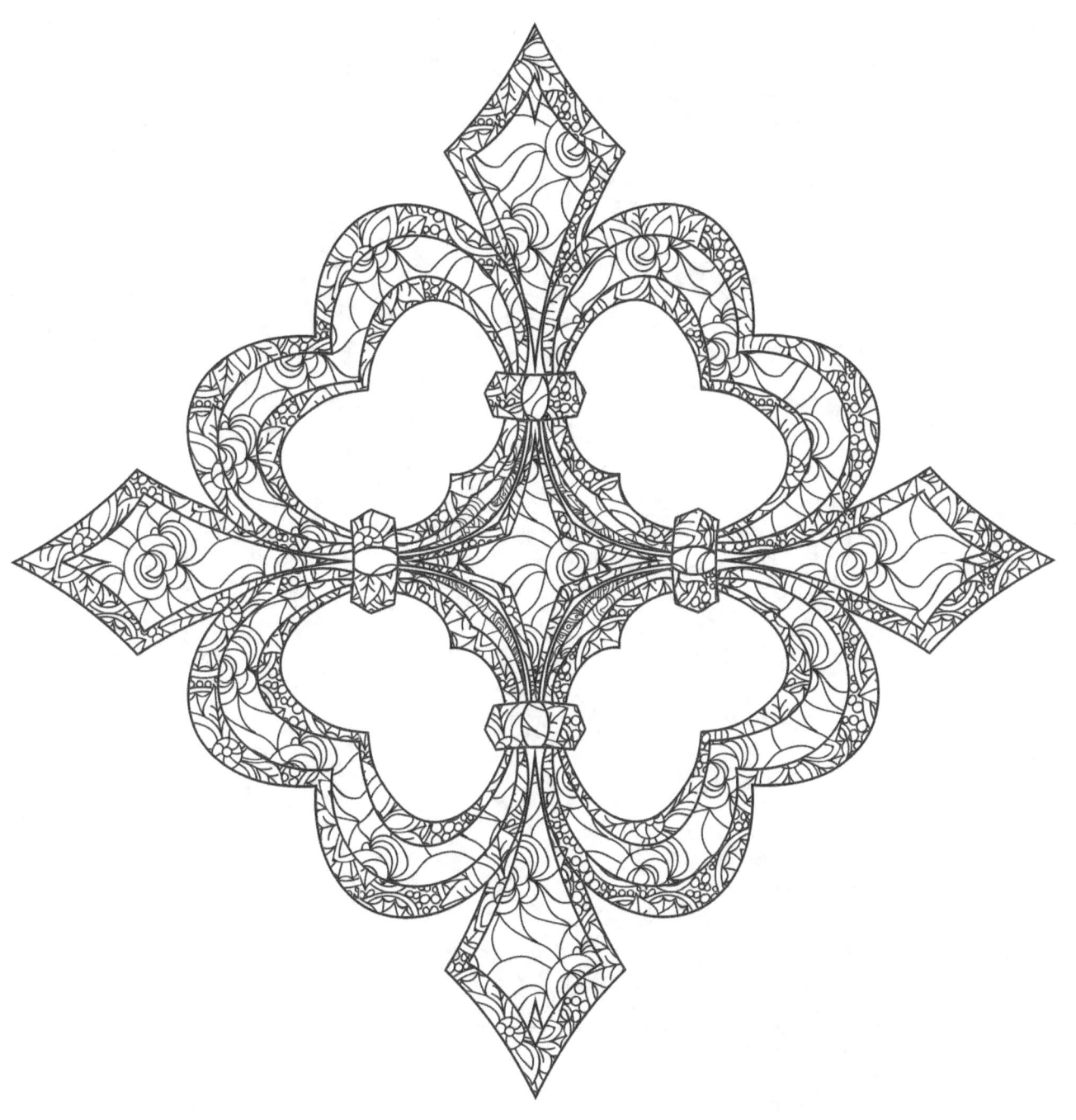

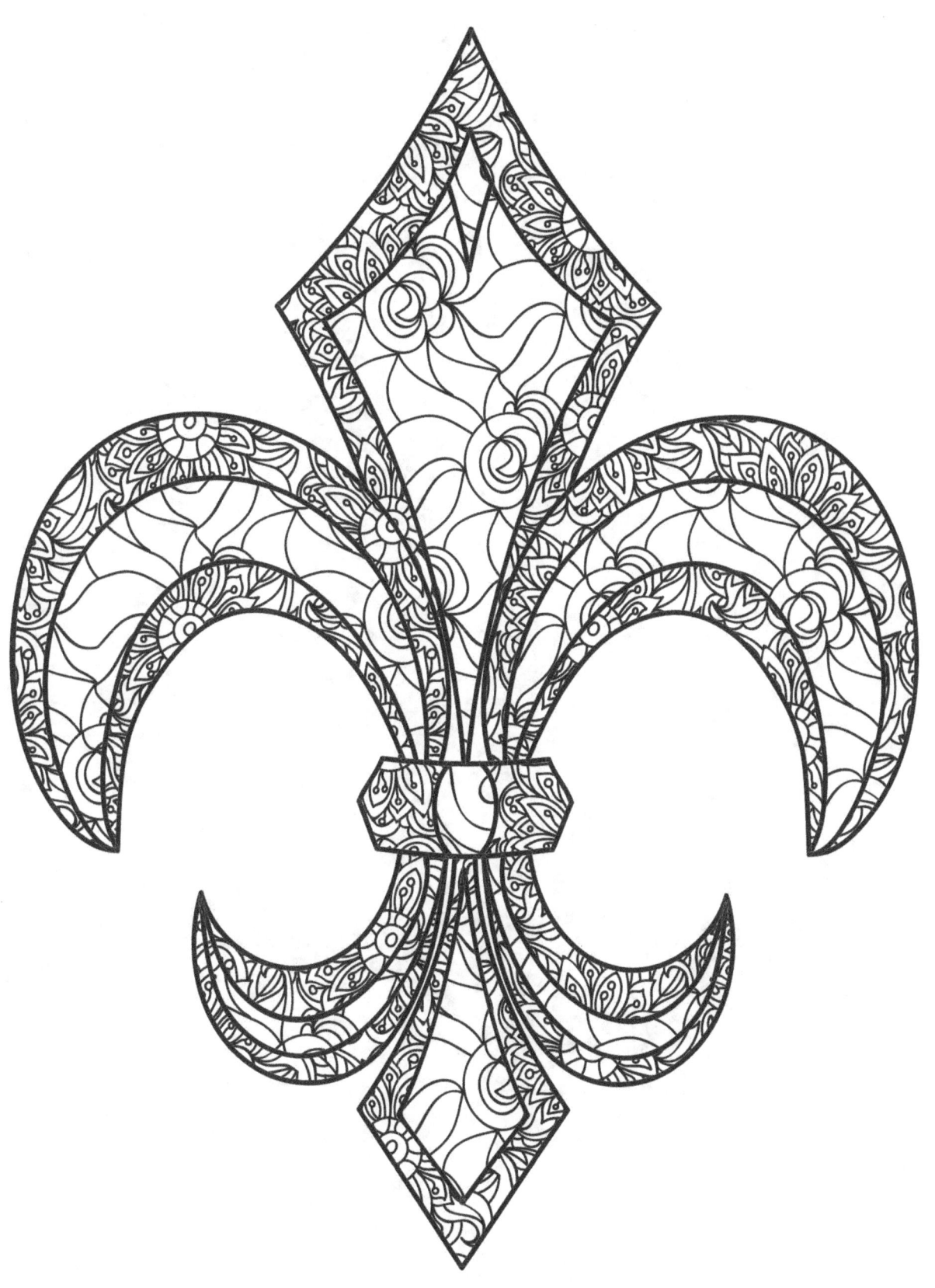

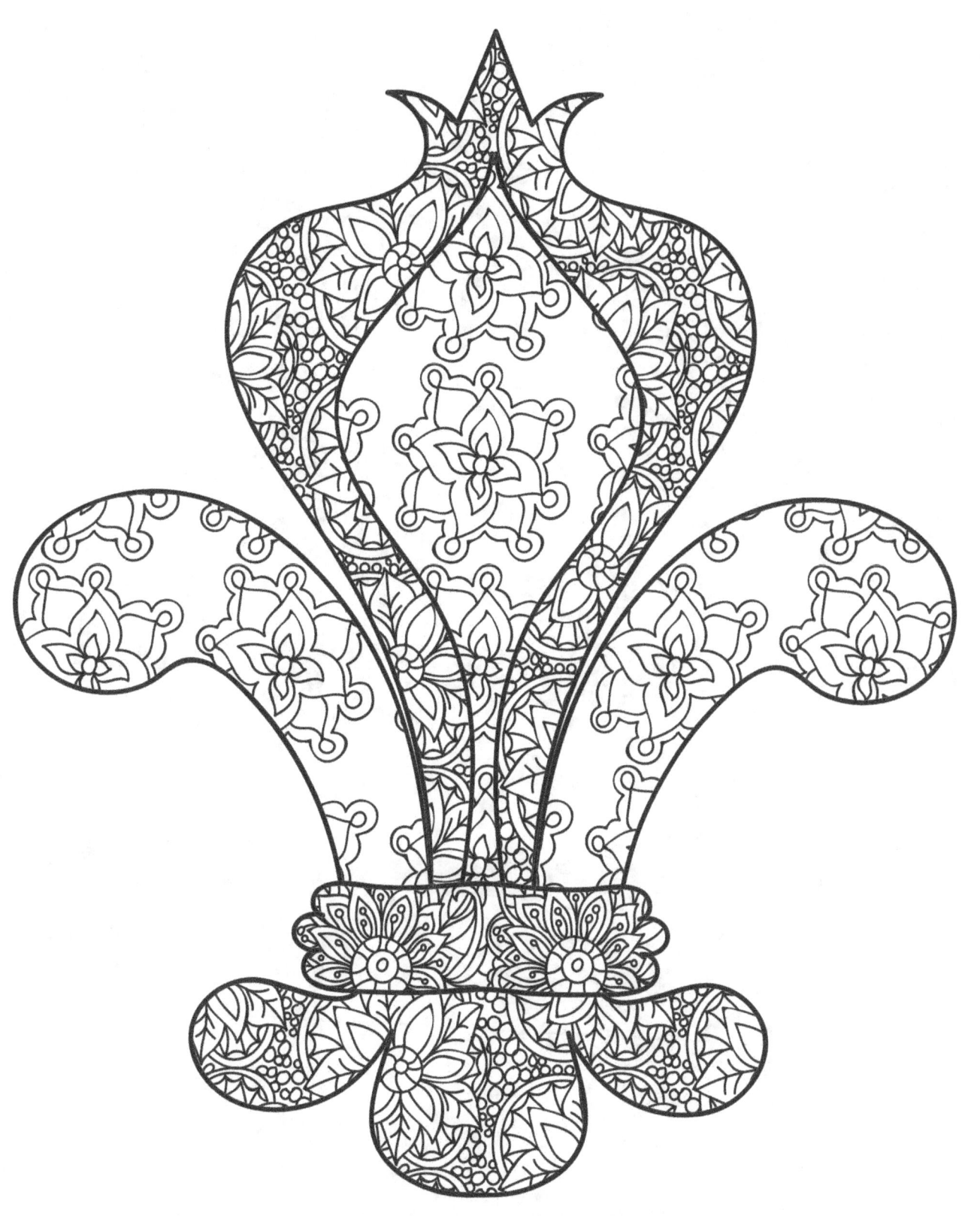

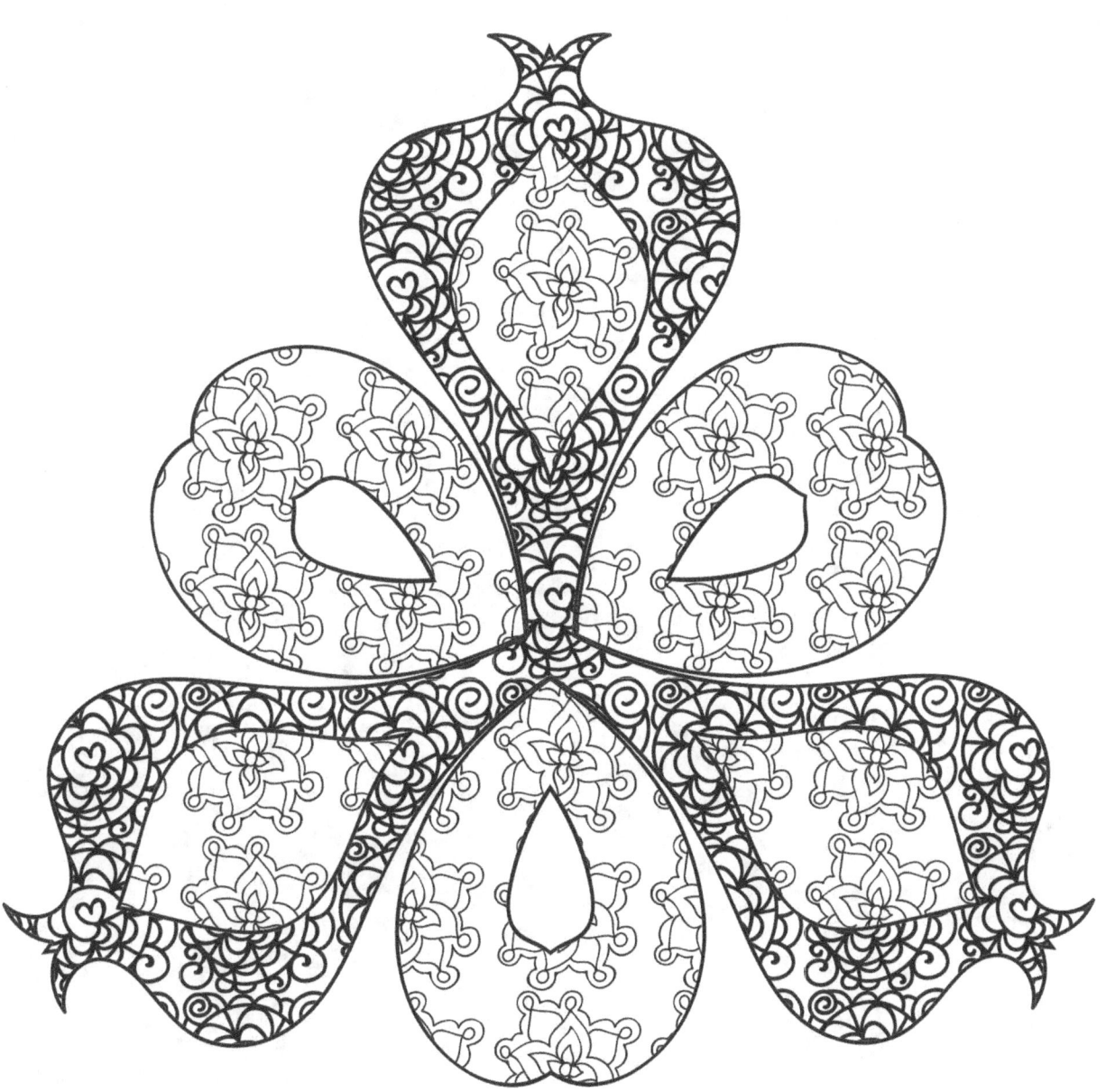

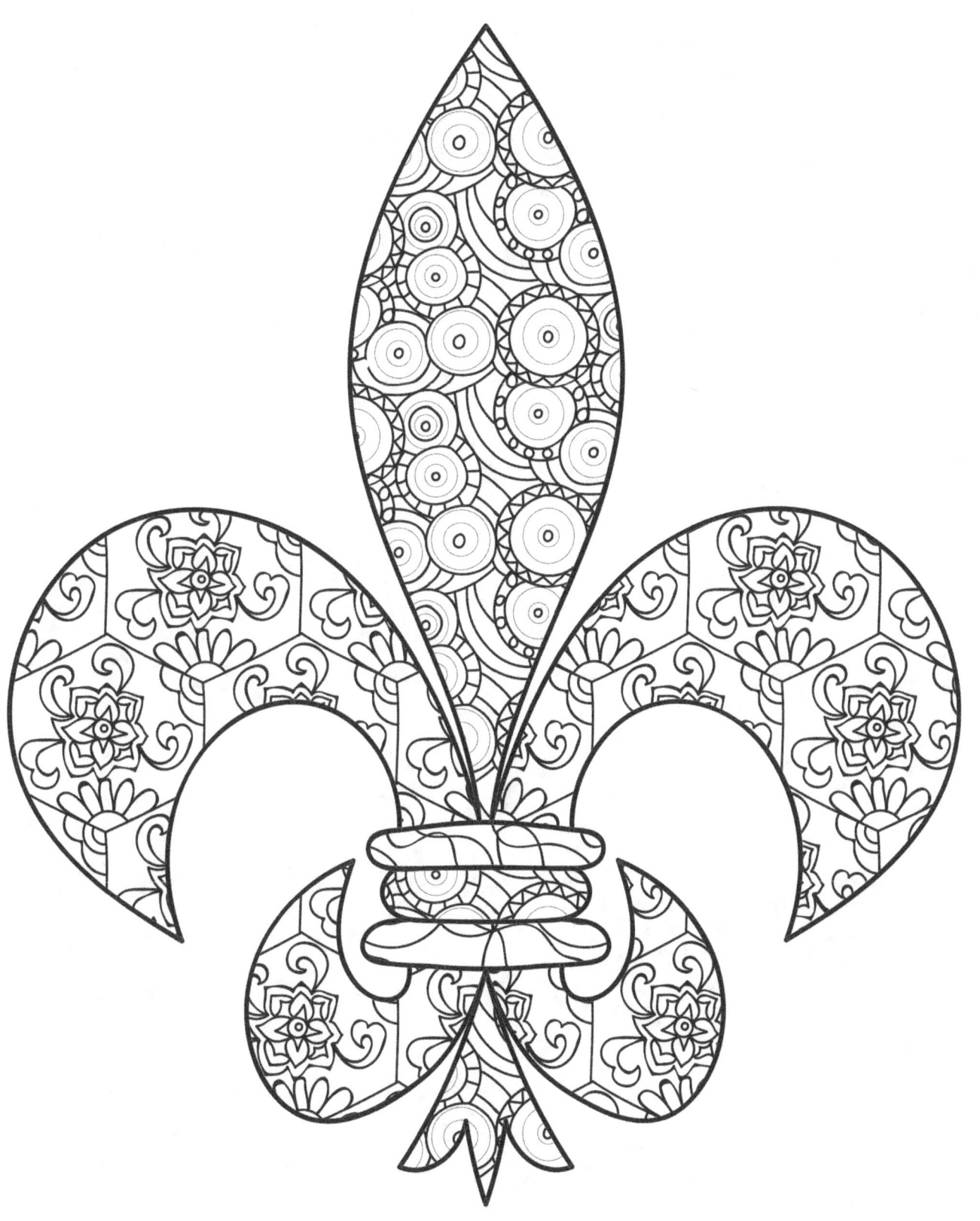

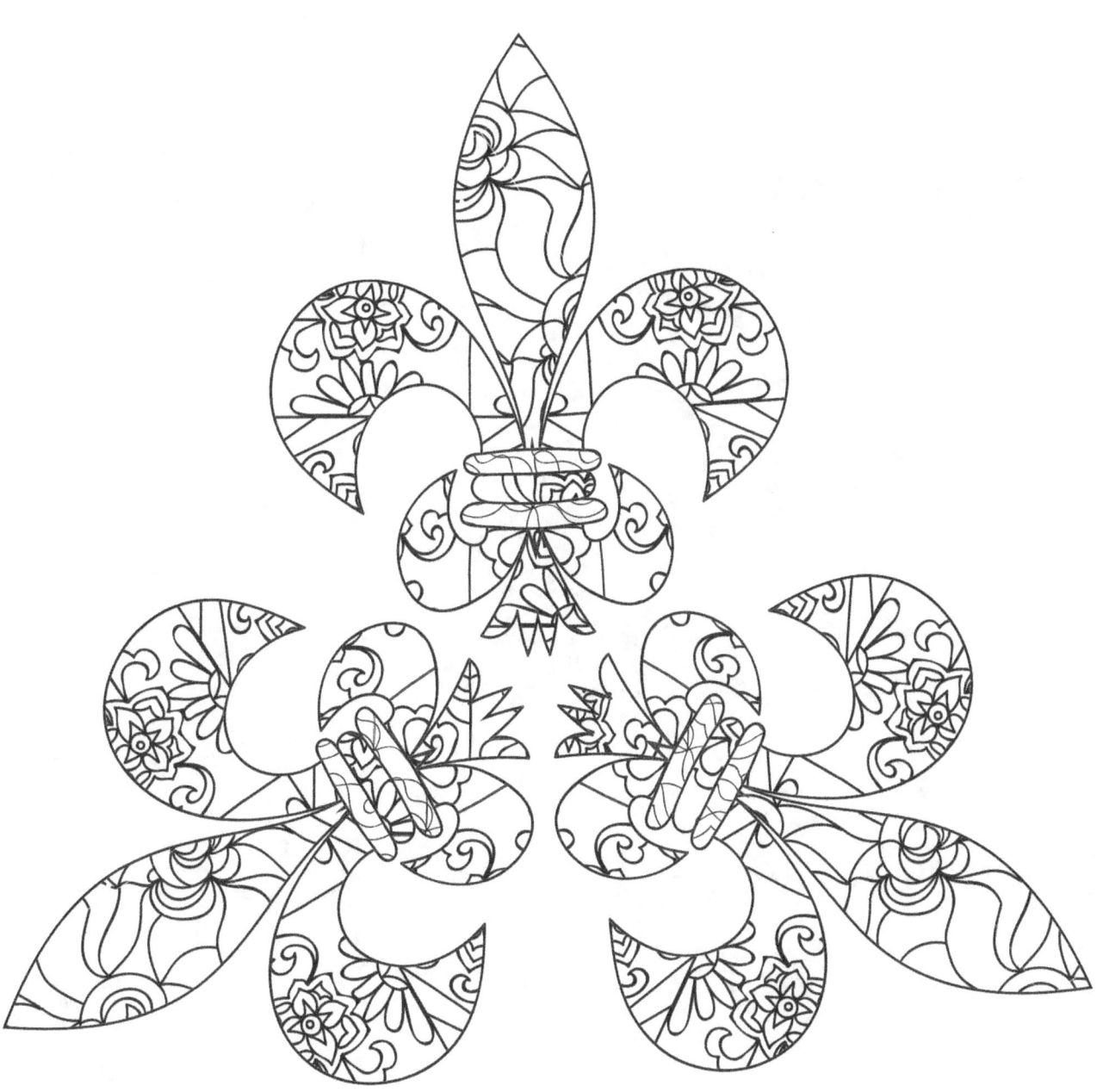

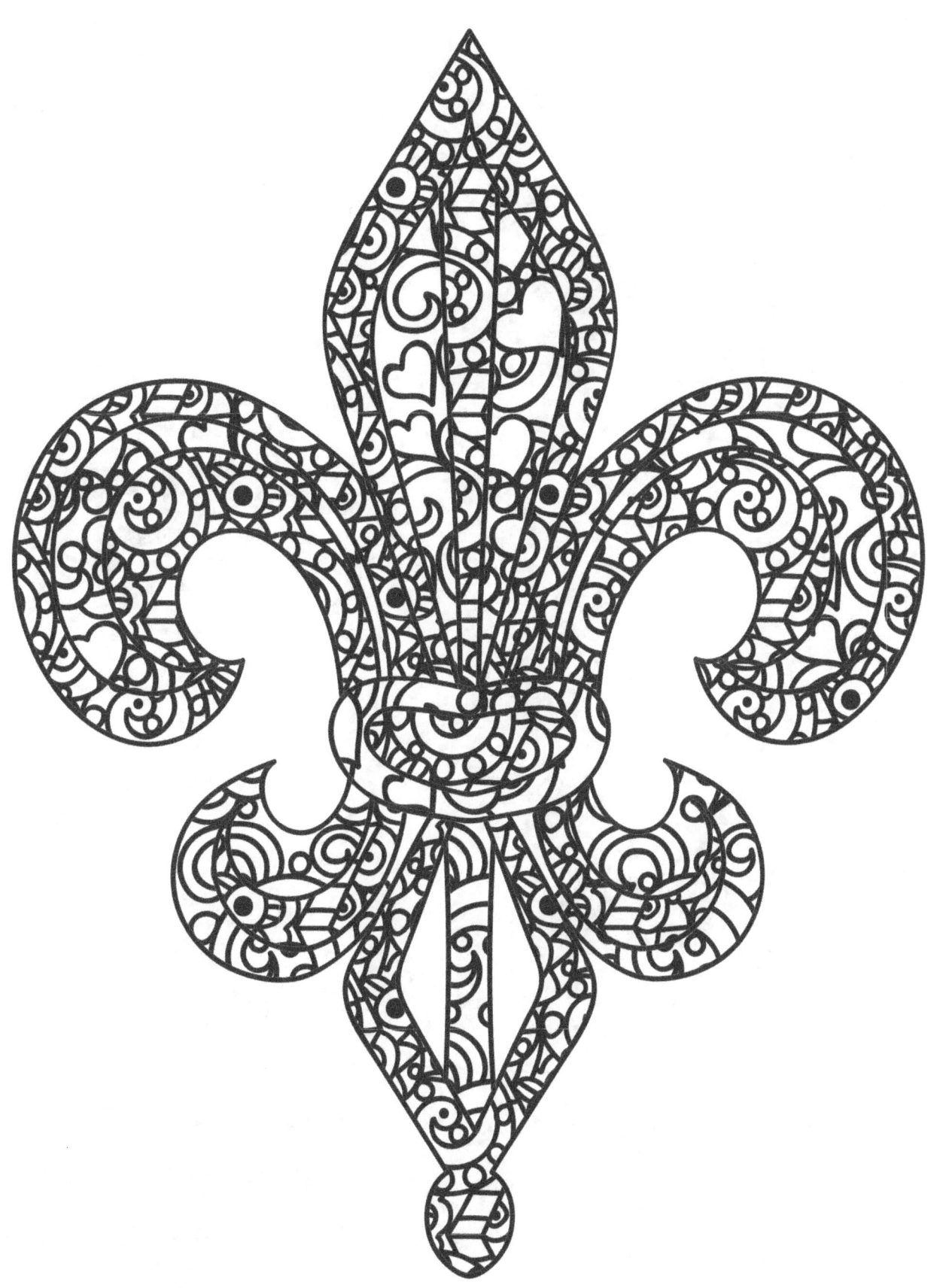

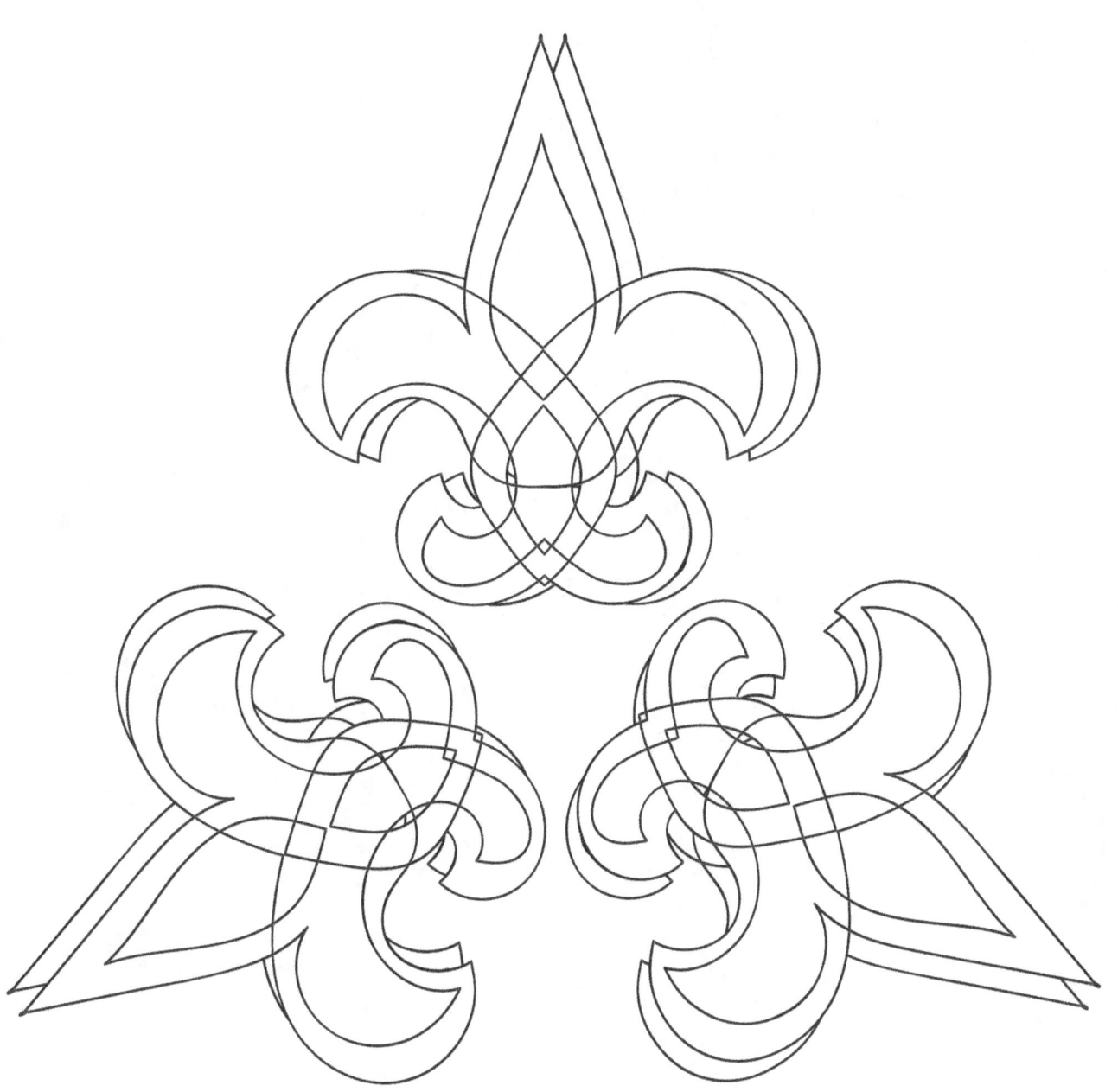

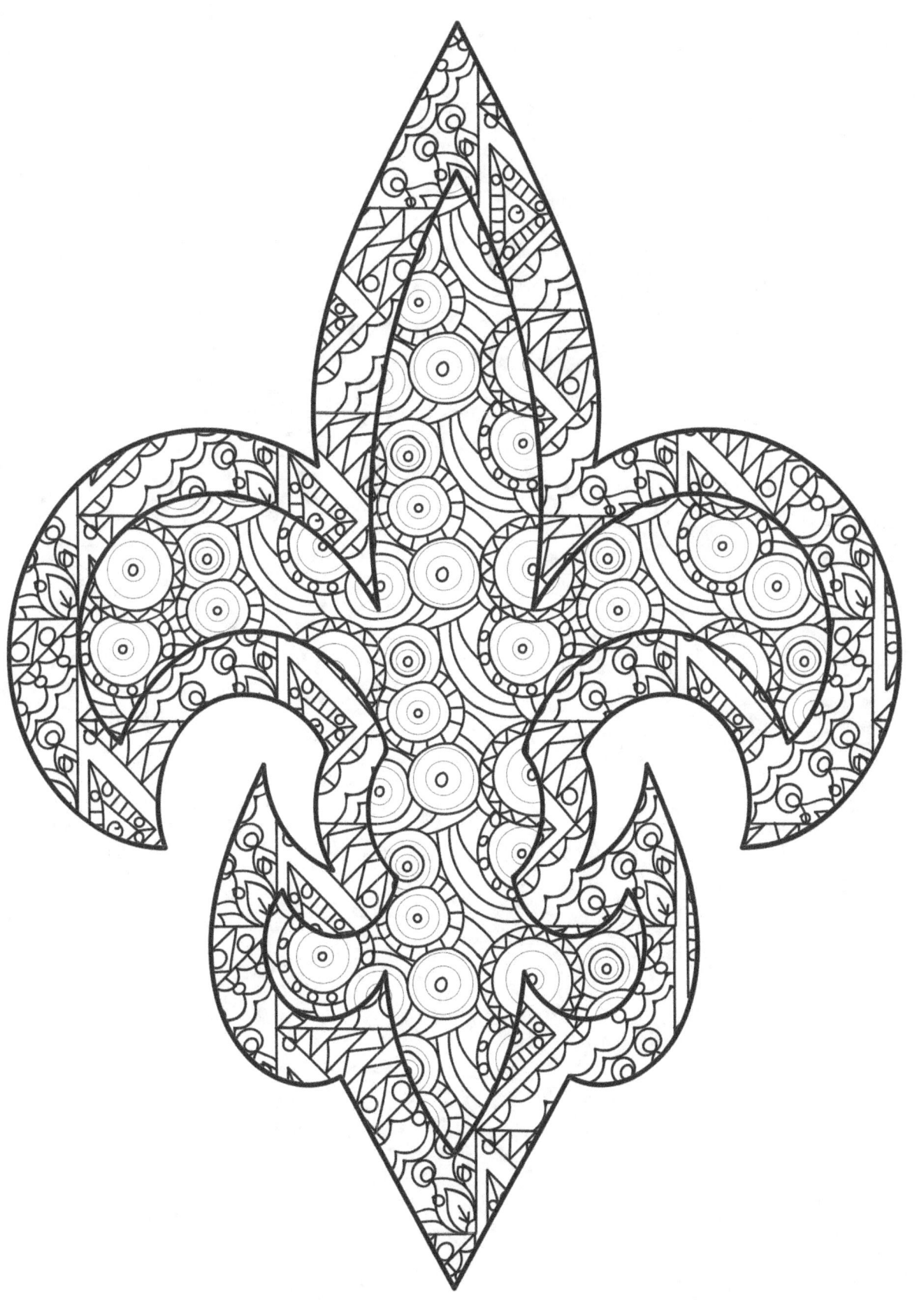

COLOR TEST PAGE

COLOR TEST PAGE

www.ingramcontent.com/pod-product-compliance
Lightning Source LLC
Chambersburg PA
CBHW081615220526
45468CB00010B/2892